*********** *ORGANIZING ON FAITH* ***********

REFLECTING
WITH SCRIPTURE ON
COMMUNITY ORGANIZING

Reverend Jeffrey K. Krehbiel

acta
PUBLICATIONS

REFLECTING WITH SCRIPTURE ON COMMUNITY ORGANIZING
by Reverend Jeffrey K. Krehbiel

Edited by Gregory F. Augustine Pierce

Cover and text design and typesetting by Patricia Lynch

Scripture quotes are from the *New Revised Standard Version of the Bible*, copyright © 1989 by the Division of Christian Education of the National Council of the Churches of Christ in the USA. All rights reserved. Used with permission.

Published by ACTA Publications, 4848 N. Clark Street, Chicago, IL 60640, (800) 397-2282, www.actapublications.com

ISBN: 0-970-87946-448-6
Printed in the United State of America by Total Printing Systems
Year 20 19 18 17 16 15 14 13 12 11 10
Printing 15 14 13 12 11 10 9 8 7 6 5 4 3 2 First Printing

♻ Text printed on 30% post-consumer recycled paper

CONTENTS

****

A Note from the Publisher
p. 5

Introduction
p. 7

Reflection One: From Crowd to Community
Mark 6:30-44
p. 11

Reflection Two: From Anger to Action
Exodus 3:1-9, 4:10-13
p. 21

Reflection Three: From Pride to Perseverance
Luke 18:1-8
p. 29

Reflection Four:
From "The World As It Is"
to "The World As It Should Be"
Isaiah 65:17-25
p. 37

Appendix
Group Study Guide
p. 45

To George Todd,
who first introduced me
to the world of organizing.

A NOTE FROM THE PUBLISHER

★ ★ ★ ★

Churches, congregations, mosques, and temples historically have been attracted to community organizing as their best way of working for social justice and the common good. Yet there has always been a tension between the "actions" of community organizations and the "values" of the religious groups, mostly revolving around issues of tactics, power, and accountability.

In recent years, many congregations have also begun using the tools of community organizing (including relational meetings, power analysis, leadership training and development, and action and evaluation) to renew and rebuild their own institutions. This has led to increased engagement and positive synergy between the two.

What is needed is a way of reflecting on the relationship, using the sacred texts and writings of the various religious traditions and the experiences gleaned from the organizing efforts of the congregations themselves. This little booklet is a fine example of how it can be done.

The author, the Rev. Dr. Jeffrey Krehbiel, is the pastor of Church of the Pilgrims in Washington, D.C., a Presbyterian Church (USA) congregation in the

Dupont Circle neighborhood. He is also co-chair of the Washington Interfaith Network, a community organization affiliated with the Industrial Areas Foundation, the oldest and largest community organizing network in the country. He has been involved in community organizing for more than twenty-five years. He offers here four reflections based on passages from the Bible and includes directions for using the reflections for group study.

ACTA Publications is committed to publishing this kind of useful, insightful, and accessible material on the connections between religious institutions of different faiths and denominations and the community organizations that respect and work with those institutions.

Gregory F. Augustine Pierce
Publisher
ACTA Publications

INTRODUCTION

★★★★

I have a friend who calls himself a "community-organizing fundamentalist." By that he means that community organizing offers the best hope not only for the renewal of American democracy, but for the renewal of the church itself.

This phrase speaks to me. I have been involved in community organizing for over twenty-five years and have come to know firsthand more than a dozen groups organized on a "broad-based" or "faith-based" model. Together, these organizations have fought to build thousands of units of affordable housing, reform troubled public schools, put police on the streets, and invest millions of dollars in city neighborhoods.

What I have learned from community organizing has helped me understand not only how any congregation or religious institution can effectively impact its local community, but also how it can strengthen its own membership at the same time. This is the unique gift that I believe church-based community organizing offers to the church.

Despite this truth, the basic vocabulary of community organizing—power, self-interest, anger, politics—is troubling to many church leaders. How often at a presbytery worship service, during the corporate prayer of confession, we are asked to disavow our preference for "the currency of power" and our "selfish ambition" while being exhorted to consider our own interests last. Jesus is understood by many church people to be a model of self-effacing humility and powerlessness, while community organizers exult in the virtue of self-interest and the necessity of power. For many Christians, the vocabulary of faith and the vocabulary of organizing seem to be at odds, if not in outright contradiction.

> **For many Christians, the vocabulary of faith and the vocabulary of organizing seem to be at odds, if not in outright contradiction.**

Over the years, not only has my faith influenced the way I organize, but organizing has influenced the way I read the Bible. If Karl Barth is right, that preaching is the art of holding the Bible in one hand and the newspaper in the other, then the interpretive task of the preacher involves bringing the experience of our daily lives to bear upon our reading of the Bible and vice versa. As I have done so, while engaged in the nitty-gritty work of organizing—conducting one-on-one individual meetings with members of my church and residents of the community, researching issues like code enforcement and tax increment financing, negotiating with public officials for affordable housing and community investment—I have discovered vistas in the Biblical text that I had not noticed before, and over time have come to see the task of organizing not only as compatible with my Christian faith, but deeply rooted in the Biblical narrative. The four reflections that follow are my attempt to engage the Bible with my experience in organizing, and engage my organizing with the Scriptures.

Each reflection is a close reading of a particular text. I have not attempted to be comprehensive in covering the Bible or exhaustive of all the various topics related to community organizing, nor am I necessarily claiming that these texts are *primarily* about community organizing. Rather what I have sought to do is to demonstrate how the Bible can illumine the work of community organizing and how organizing can create a window into the Biblical text. My hope is that these experiments will prove helpful not only to church leaders who are new to organizing and perhaps struggling to reconcile their faith with the vocabulary of organizing, but also to veteran leaders who may not always read the Bible with an organizing lens. I hope they will be helpful as well to community organizers who may not know the Christian Scriptures well.

I write this book as a Christian pastor, aware that most organizing does (and should) take place in an interfaith context. I hope this work might inspire others to do similar work from within their own faith tradition. I, for example, would love to have an Imam or a Muslim community organizer walk me through passages of the Koran. I can say the same of the foundational texts of the other great religious and philosophical movements.

In the appendix, I have included study guides on each of the four reflections so that the texts can be explored more fully in a group context. I trust that my insights into the text will be useful, but it is more powerful for people to wrestle directly with the text themselves and come to their own conclusions.

Each of these passages has been explored by me with others in group Bible studies, and I could not have written what I have without the insights that came from the many individuals and groups that wrestled with these texts with me. The intent of this book, like any book that focuses on the Bible, is to encourage the reader to look again at the Scriptures with fresh eyes. The power of sacred texts always outstrips our capacity to contain them, and I am confident that groups that explore any of these Bible passages together will discover far more than I have been able to capture in these pages.

Rev. Dr. Jeffrey Krehbiel
Pastor, Church of the Pilgrims
Washington, D.C.

REFLECTION ONE
FROM CROWD TO COMMUNITY

* * * *

MARK 6:30-44

[When they returned] the apostles gathered around Jesus, and told him all that they had done and taught. He said to them, "Come away to a deserted place all by yourselves and rest a while." For many were coming and going, and they had no leisure even to eat. And they went away in the boat to a deserted place by themselves. Now many saw them going and recognized them, and they hurried there on foot from all the towns and arrived ahead of them. As Jesus went ashore, he saw a great crowd; and he had compassion for them, because they were like sheep without a shepherd; and he began to teach them many things.

When it grew late, his disciples came to him and said, "This is a deserted place, and the hour is now very late; send them away so that they may go into the surrounding country and villages and buy something for themselves to eat." But he answered them, "You give them something to eat." They said to him, "Are we to go and buy two hundred denarii worth of bread, and give it to them to eat?" And he said to them, "How many loaves have you? Go and see." When they had found out, they said, "Five, and two fish."

Then he ordered them to get all the people to sit down in groups on the green grass. So they sat down in groups of hundreds and of fifties. Taking the five loaves and the two fish, he looked up to heaven, and blessed and broke the loaves, and gave them to his disciples to set before the people; and he divided the two fish among them all. And all ate and were filled; and they took up twelve baskets full of broken pieces and of the fish. Those who had eaten the loaves numbered five thousand men.

You can hardly blame the disciples for being a little irritated with Jesus. Here they have just returned from their first missionary adventure, weary yet bursting with energy to share with him "all they have done and taught." In response, Jesus invites them to go away with him "to a deserted place by themselves" (Mark repeats this twice for emphasis). The first-ever-recorded church retreat is interrupted, however, in part because of the success of their own outreach. The crowd sees them going, recognizes them, and follows them. The disciples, together with Jesus, have begun to establish relationships with the people, and they are no longer anonymous.

When Jesus sees the throng amassed on the shoreline, he is moved to compassion and cancels (or at least postpones) the retreat. For him, it is time to get to work. We can imagine that the disciples had a somewhat different reaction. By the time night falls, they are both frustrated with Jesus and fatigued by the work. In context, Jesus' response to their rather sensible suggestion to send the crowd away seems almost incomprehensible: "*You* give them something to eat." The crowd has now become a burden.

Their burden.

Yet that seems not to be what Jesus has in mind. The disciples assume the resources for this repast must come only from them. Jesus instead sends them into the midst of the people to assess what resources might be available from those they are called to serve. They are not impressed by what they discover, but Jesus is not dissuaded. What they have will be enough.

Then, in a move that is often overlooked in the retelling, Jesus prompts the disciples to act in a way that they must have found mystifying at the time. He directs them to have the crowd sit down in groups on the green grass. Not just any size groups, but groups of fifty and one hundred. In that moment, the crowd becomes a community. Then, to reinforce their role as leaders, after blessing and breaking the loaves and the fish, Jesus gives the food to the disciples to set before the people. It is they, not he, who feed them.

Without diminishing the miracle, notice how fundamentally this move alters the dynamic of the narrative.

You can visualize the significance of the transformation. I picture a supply truck arriving in a refugee camp, the hungry crowd gathering as a frenzied pack to get their share of the scarce resources before they quickly disappear. In community, the dynamics are altogether different. Sitting in a circle, you connect with those around you. As you pass the bread from person to person, aware of how many people it has to feed, you are less likely to take more than your share, both because you can see the faces of those around you and because the collective will of the group would not allow anything else. You can imagine—though Mark does not say it—that those who might have had a little extra tucked away, afraid to share with the hungry crowd, now are more willing to add theirs to the collective pot, knowing that there will be enough for them, too.

Everyone in the story learns something before the day is done. The disciples assume that the hungry crowd is helpless and must either be dispersed with their needs ignored or become dependent on the social service of the disciples. Jesus teaches them instead how to organize the crowd into a community and how to look more deeply to discover the abundant resources already present—resources the crowd itself may not have known existed. From the outset, the disciples see the crowd as *their* burden, a drain on *their* energy, and a responsibility beyond *their* capabilities. Jesus demonstrates how even the disciples' own needs are met when they trust the resourcefulness of those with whom they are in ministry. Lest this point be lost, Mark drives it home in the final verse. The weary and hungry disciples, who at the start "have no leisure even to eat," at the end collect twelve baskets full of broken pieces of bread and fish—one basket for each of them!

This is the basic dynamic of organizing.

The Quaker writer Parker Palmer has suggested that the tension in the story—and the tension in our culture—is between what biblical scholar Walter Brueggemann calls the "myth of scarcity and the liturgy of abundance." The worry over scarcity drives the disciples to doubt their own leadership, to discount the crowd's resources, to want to send the people away, and to imagine that their needs will be met only if each person fends for himself or herself. The myth of scarcity leads to isolation.

The liturgy of abundance is celebrated in community. Jesus pushes the disciples into relationship. Their leadership is still critical; it is they who organize the crowd into groups. But it is in relationship in the context of community that the resources flow.

So it is in organizing: Leaders learn the art of the "individual, one-to-one, relational meeting," leaving the safe confines of hearth and home to forge relationships across social divides. And, as happened to the disciples, out of community comes common action. Whereas in social outreach ministries, churches often meet neighbors at the point of their need—through food pantries and soup kitchens and shelters—in organizing, relationships are formed at the point of strength.

The Iron Rule of organizing is "Never do for others what they can do for themselves." Organizers enter a community not to catalogue a litany of the community's deficits, but to identify and train leaders. A fundamental assumption of organizing is that every community has within it leaders capable of acting on their own behalf in relationship with others. The goal of organizing is to find and cultivate those leaders.

> **A fundamental assumption of organizing is that every community has within it leaders capable of acting on their own behalf in relationship with others.**

This is a lesson that leaders, in and out of the church, must learn and relearn again and again.

Most church leaders know the experience of feeling as if everything depended on them, and all have had moments at least when the needs of the congregation feel like a burden. Leaders and managers in the corporate and nonprofit world know the same experience. The myth of scarcity leads us to imagine that we are the only ones with leadership skills, and—again like the disciples—to assume that the only options are to send people away with their needs unmet or to have them depend upon us alone.

Perhaps in a misguided attempt to please those we serve, clergy are often the worst violators of the Iron

Rule. We are constantly doing for others what they are fully capable of doing for themselves. Congregations do the same thing. We assume that the most "Christ-like" thing we can do in the community outside our door is to identify a need and then meet it.

For most congregations, organizing requires a fundamental reorientation of our approach. The community around the church has resources, not just needs, and our role in organizing is to help identify them.

Mark's narrative invites us to abandon our assumptions of scarcity and trust the abundant resources of the communities in which we serve, both inside and outside the congregation. While there are certainly times when going on retreat is appropriate and getting away to a deserted place by ourselves is just what the doctor ordered, Jesus refuses to let the needs of the crowd be ignored because that is our need. If we come to feel that it all depends upon us, then the recourse is not to escape for a time, only to return so that once again we can be the sole provider of leadership in our congregations and communities, but to look more deeply, to "go and see" what resources are present that we have not yet discovered. The promise of community, and the testimony of organizing, is that we will discover resources in such abundance that not only will the community discover its capacity to meet its own needs, but our own spirits will be fed in the process. At the end of the day, there is a basket for each one of us, too.

In Mark's story, Jesus gives the disciples the authority to organize the crowd. He tells them to have the people sit down in groups on the green grass. In our communities today it is not always clear who has such authority. There was a time in American culture when many groups—political parties, unions, community associations—were at work organizing people for collective action, identifying and developing leadership. Today, in most of our urban areas and increasingly in our rural and suburban communities as well, organizing work takes place in a vacuum. In the majority of our communities, no one is fulfilling the basic mandate of Jesus' task to "go and see what you have."

In this vacuum, faith-based community organizing dares to claim for itself such authority to act. In hundreds of communities across the country, leaders of church and synagogue are sitting down in church basements, in neighbors' living rooms, in neighborhood coffee shops to ask the most basic questions out of which community may emerge: "What are your dreams for the community in which you live? What would you do to make things better? Are you willing to join together with others so that we might work to change the way things are?"

We do so not to advance the agenda of the church, but to discover and actualize the agenda of the community. At the start of such work, resources often appear meager, like the five loaves and two fish. The liturgy of abundance invites us to trust that out of such meager resources miracles can happen.

REFLECTION QUESTIONS

- Where do you see the tension between scarcity and abundance involved in your church and community work? Describe it.

- How, specifically, would things change if you operated on the liturgy of abundance instead of the myth of scarcity?

REFLECTION TWO

FROM ANGER TO ACTION

★ ★ ★ ★

EXODUS 3:1-9, 4:10-13

Moses was keeping the flock of his father-in-law Jethro, the priest of Midian; he led his flock beyond the wilderness, and came to Horeb, the mountain of God. There the angel of the LORD appeared to him in a flame of fire out of a bush; he looked, and the bush was blazing, yet it was not consumed. Then Moses said, "I must turn aside and look at this great sight, and see why the bush is not burned up." When the LORD saw that he had turned aside to see, God called to him out of the bush, "Moses, Moses!" And he said, "Here I am." Then he said, "Come no closer! Remove the sandals from your feet, for the place on which you are standing is holy ground." He said further, "I am the God of your father, the God of Abraham, the God of Isaac, and the God of Jacob." And Moses hid his face, for he was afraid to look at God. Then the LORD said, "I have observed the misery of my people who are in Egypt; I have

21

heard their cry on account of their taskmasters. Indeed, I know their sufferings, and I have come down to deliver them from the Egyptians, and to bring them up out of that land to a good and broad land, a land flowing with milk and honey, to the country of the Canaanites, the Hittites, the Amorites, the Perizzites, the Hivites, and the Jebusites. The cry of the Israelites has now come to me; I have also seen how the Egyptians oppress them.

So come, I will send you to Pharaoh to bring my people, the Israelites, out of Egypt." But Moses said to God, "Who am I that I should go to Pharaoh, and bring the Israelites out of Egypt?" He said, "I will be with you; and this shall be the sign for you that it is I who sent you: when you have brought the people out of Egypt, you shall worship God on this mountain...."

But Moses said to the LORD, "O my Lord, I have never been eloquent, neither in the past nor even now that you have spoken to your servant; but I am slow of speech and slow of tongue." Then the LORD said to him, "Who gives speech to mortals? Who makes them mute or deaf, seeing or blind? Is it not I, the LORD? Now go, and I will be with your mouth and teach you what you are to speak." But Moses said, "O my Lord, please send someone else."

If the first task of organizing is to identify and train leaders, what sort of leaders do organizers look for? What are the qualities that make for a leader? The Bible is replete with stories of God calling people into leadership, and many of these stories bear the marks of organizing. Perhaps the best organizing story in the Bible is Israel's foundational narrative found in the book of Exodus. As a story, it has it all: an oppressive ruler, a dramatic story of birth and rescue, palace intrigue, clever midwives, confrontation, despair, and—ultimately—liberation. Through it all is the activity of this inscrutable God who has "observed the misery of my people" and resolves to act. Yet God does not act alone. If YHWH is the initiator in the story, Moses is the reluctant protagonist.

Given Moses' noted limitations ("I have never been eloquent, neither in the past nor even now") and his obvious hesitation ("please send someone else"), why would God choose Moses to go to Pharaoh in the first place? There are several good reasons suggested by the narrative. His unique experience as a Hebrew child growing up in Pharaoh's palace gives him both access to the palace and an understanding of the Pharaoh's inner circle. Surely such knowledge would serve him well in his task to speak truth to power. We learn, as the narrative unfolds, of Moses' steadfastness despite frustrations and setbacks. In any struggle for change, persistence is an essential attribute. Organizers, however, might suggest another quality of Moses' character that may have been paramount: Moses was angry. As Jesus would describe such people in his Sermon on the Mount, Moses hungered and thirsted for justice.

You will recall the reason Moses is in the wilderness in the first place is because he was a fugitive from Pharaoh's death squads. Witnessing the Egyptian overseer beating the Hebrew slave moved Moses to homicidal anger. The next day his anger is provoked yet again when he observes two Hebrew slaves fighting with one another. The narration of these two episodes is brief and without commentary. Yet together they convey something important in Israel's collective memory about the character of Moses. A child of privilege, he nonetheless recognizes the injustice inflicted upon his own kinsfolk. Their oppression, however, does not blind him to their own faults or diminish his capacity to call his own people to account.

> **If you cannot remember what you really value, if you do not grieve over the way things are that do not respect those values, you cannot sustain the struggle to organize for change.**

Lots of good church folks wrestle with the appropriateness of organizing around anger at injustice. It somehow is presented as the antithesis of what should motivate the hearts of good church people. Organizers, however, point out that the word anger derives from the Old Norse word meaning "memory" or "grief." Healthy anger is deeply related to loss—loss of one's past that has been taken away, loss of potential for what might be. Anger, therefore, is a necessary prerequisite for leadership. If you cannot remember what you really value, if you do not grieve over the way things are that do not respect those values, you cannot sustain the struggle to organize for change.

In his book, *Roots for Radicals*, the long-time executive director of the Industrial Areas Foundation (IAF), Ed Chambers, references a document drafted by African American clergy in the IAF, that reads in part:

> *Anger and grief are rooted in our most passionate memories and dreams—a father whose spirit has been broken by demeaning work or no work; a brother or sister lost to violence or alcohol or drugs; a church burned down by an arsonist; a college career sabotaged by a substandard high school; a neighborhood of shops and families and affections and relationships ripped apart because banks wouldn't lend to it, because insurance companies wouldn't insure it, because city officials wouldn't service it, because youth wouldn't respect it, because teachers wouldn't teach in it. Anger sits precariously between two dangerous extremes. One extreme is hatred, the breeding ground of violence. The other extreme is passivity and apathy, the breeding ground of despair and living death. Anger that is focused and deep and rooted in grief is a key element in the organizing of black churches.*

So in the Exodus narrative, Moses' just anger is the thread that sustains his leadership: his anger at Pharaoh for his oppressive policies; his anger at the Hebrew people for their passivity before Pharaoh, their longing to return to Egypt, their impatience with his leadership; his anger at Aaron for his idolatry of the golden calf; even his anger at God for getting him into the middle of this mess in the first place. What God does, in essence, is to redeem Moses' anger, to redirect it, to harness it for God's purposes so that it becomes the goad that drives his leadership and leads to the liberation of the Hebrew people.

God's encounter with Moses, like all relationships, began with a direct, personal encounter. God calls Moses by name. God credentials himself with reference to Moses' family of origin ("I am the God of your father, the God of Abraham, the God of Isaac, and the God of Jacob"). God taps into Moses' own memory and grief by acknowledging the reality of the situation in which Moses now finds himself ("I have observed the misery of my people who are in Egypt; I have heard their cry on account of their taskmasters"). God challenges Moses to act ("I will send you to Pharaoh to bring my people, the Israelites, out of Egypt").

So when organizers and leaders enter a community, they engage people in conversations about what matters most in their lives. What are their passions, their hopes, their dreams? What have been the experiences that shaped their values and character? What sort of future do they want for themselves and their families? How do they cope with the daily frustrations of life in their community? What actions have they taken in their lives to make change? How are they in relationship with those who live around them? Are they willing to work with others to forge a different sort of future? Are they in touch with their own reservoir of anger—memory and grief—so that they might take the necessary risks required to build the sort of relational power that can make real change happen?

REFLECTION QUESTIONS

- How do you understand the qualities of a good leader? Name them. Give an example of someone who exhibits them.

- How do memory and grief play a role in your own church and community work? Be specific.

REFLECTION THREE
FROM PRIDE TO PERSEVERANCE

★★★★

LUKE 18:1-8

Then Jesus told them a parable about their need to pray always and not to lose heart. He said, "In a certain city there was a judge who neither feared God nor had respect for people. In that city there was a widow who kept coming to him and saying, 'Grant me justice against my opponent.' For a while he refused; but later he said to himself, 'Though I have no fear of God and no respect for anyone, yet because this widow keeps bothering me, I will grant her justice, so that she may not wear me out by continually coming.'" And the Lord said, "Listen to what the unjust judge says. And will not God grant justice to his chosen ones who cry to him day and night? Will he delay long in helping them? I tell you, he will quickly grant justice to them. And yet, when the Son of Man comes, will he find faith on earth?"

It's not exactly clear to me how *pride* was first identified as one of the cardinal sins in the Christian tradition with *humility* the primary *virtue*. It began, I suppose, with Augustine and his seeming preference for the writings of the Apostle Paul over the teachings of Jesus, and his focus on his own experience as part of the all-male hierarchy of the church (following in the footsteps of the Emperor Constantine, for whom pride was often the vice of choice). Nevertheless, it's hard to read the gospels and see humility as Jesus' most important attribute. Time and again, Jesus praises strong, outrageous action: blind Bartimaeus who calls out to him from the side of the road, much to the consternation of Jesus' disciples; the woman with the flow of blood who breaks taboo to touch him in the midst of the crowd; the Syro-Phoenician woman who argues with Jesus about the welfare of her daughter until he relents and sends her on her way; the four friends who literally tear the roof off the house to present their friend to Jesus for healing. In each case, Jesus pronounces, "Your faith has made you well."

True, Jesus also said "You must take up your cross and follow me," but not once did he say to anyone who came to him for healing, "Your ailment is just a cross you are going to have to bear." Not once did he imply that disability was simply our lot in life or a punishment for our sins or those of our forebears. Nowhere does he suggest to those who are poor or hurting or oppressed that they accept their condition or accommodate themselves to the injustice of the world.

Culminating Jesus' preference for outrageous action is this text from the Gospel of Luke, in which he tells a parable about prayer that features an annoying widow who pesters an unjust judge until he gives her what she wants. A literal translation of the Greek has the judge saying, "I will grant her justice so that she will stop battering me." And the punch line is, "When the Human One [the Son of Man] comes, will he find such faith on earth?" What sort of faith is Jesus talking about? Faith like the widow, who keeps on battering the judge until she gets what she wants. Faith like the Syro-Phoenician woman, who won't take no for an answer. Faith like Bartimaeus, who won't be silenced by Jesus' impatient disciples. Faith like the friends of the paralytic, who tore the roof right off the house.

Frederick Douglass famously said, "Power concedes nothing without a demand. It never did and it never will." In that sense, community organizing embodies Jesus' parable. The widow is wholly without power. A woman alone in a male-ordered culture, she had few individual rights of her own. In the Hebrew Scriptures, the widow, along with the orphan and the sojourner, are singled out as categories of people who deserve particular care within the community of faith. That is because the system is stacked against them. The most likely cause for the woman's suit before the judge would have been the rights to her husband's estate. It was not uncommon for unscrupulous executors to leave the widow with nothing. It is not an exaggeration to say that this case may well have been an issue of life and death for her.

For the judge, on the other hand, it was just another routine matter. Though a person of status and power, he was just a cog in a system that was designed to maintain the privilege of those like him. His role was to dismiss the woman's complaint and strike a deal with her adversary. She might make a bit of a fuss, but that's how things were done, and no one would have expected a different outcome.

Yet the widow refuses to play her assigned role. Unable to compete in the back-room negotiations that would have been available to her opponent, she takes her case public. In a culture in which she had no voice, she refuses to keep silent. She badgers the judge—and here the Greek has a certain amount of irony: The word used means to "give a black eye," a term related to boxing. In other words, the poor, beleaguered judge complains that the little old widow is beating him up!

The widow doesn't attack the judge's motives or credibility. She simply insists that he do the right thing. She badgers and batters him until he gives in. And he finally does, not because she was right, not because it is the just thing to do, not because he is worried about what God might think of his behavior, not because he is suddenly converted by the force of her argument. No. He relents because he is tired of her constant complaining and just wants her to go away.

In the arsenal of tools available to community organizations, persistence and public exposure are two of most potent weapons. Many are the times that public officials have caved to the demands of a community organization not because the organization was full of good people who cared about justice, but simply because the officials wanted to be left alone. That has been one of the most important lessons I have learned in community organizing. I used to believe that ideas matter. Well, they do matter. But having a good idea isn't enough; being right isn't enough, being on the side of the poor and oppressed isn't enough. If you aren't willing to fight, you will quickly find that Frederick Douglass was right on target: Power concedes nothing without a demand; it never has and it never will.

> **Persistence and public exposure are two of most potent weapons.**

It is astonishing, but Jesus commends such uppity behavior in our prayer life. One of the gifts of organizing for people of faith is that we learn how to pray in a new way. There is, to be sure, such a thing as selfish prayer. And there is something to be said for prayer as listening for the voice of God. Sometimes silent prayer is the best prayer you can give. In the very next story in Luke's Gospel, Jesus lauds the tax collector who prayed, "Have mercy on me, a sinner," while criticizing the Pharisee, who prayed, "Thank God I'm not like this miserable tax collector." But you would be hard-pressed to find any instruction from Jesus suggesting that prayer should be something quiet and passive. He makes it clear that our prayer life should emulate the same outrageous action as the widow, prayer that keeps pounding away until the kingdom comes.

In his book, *Luke*, the preacher Fred Craddock, who teaches at Candler School of Theology in Atlanta, comments on the relationship between this parable and our own experience of waiting for justice to come:

> *The human experience is one of delay, and honesty says as much, even while acknowledging the mystery of God's ways. Is the petitioner being hammered through long days and nights of prayer into a vessel that will be able to hold the answer when it comes? We do not know. All we know in the life of prayer is asking, seeking, knocking, and waiting, trust sometimes fainting, sometimes growing angry. Persons of such prayer life can only wonder at those who speak of prayer with the smiling facility of someone drawing answers from a hat. In a large gathering of persons concerned about certain unfair and oppressive conditions in our society, an elderly African American minister read this parable and gave a one-sentence interpretation: "Until you have stood for years knocking at a locked door, your knuckles bleeding, you do not really know what prayer is."*

Such outrageous action, such uppity faith, such tenacity, is not the norm for most of us—in or out of the church. To adopt the faith of this tenacious woman is to push ourselves beyond our comfort zone, to take risky action, to discover gifts that we did not yet know we had, to move beyond socially constructed ways of being in the world. Jesus' listeners understood full well how poor widows were expected to behave, and this widow that Jesus imagines is clearly having none of it. She is an older, single woman, alone in the world with nothing to call her own, in a culture that would have made her entirely dependent on the resources of others. Yet she refuses to play the role that society has assigned for her. She refuses to go along. She stands up for herself, and does not back down.

You know the trendy phrase about finding our "inner child"? Perhaps what we need to do is to find our "inner widow." We probably all have a pretty good idea about what gets our hackles up. What are the injustices in our world that really burn you? See if you can channel this widow, then spend a week in prayer loudly complaining to God about what you know is wrong in the world, and see if you aren't a changed person by the time the week is done. By the end of the week, I imagine that it will no longer matter whether you have the perfect gifts, whether you are just the right person, whether you have heard a clear enough call. Instead, you will be in touch with your very own God-given passion. The only thing that will matter to you is that there is something to be done and you can no longer just sit on the sidelines and watch.

That's the faith the Human One will be looking for when he returns to this earth. And the place to begin is in prayer. Pray always, Jesus tell us, and don't lose heart. Like the widow, if we pray always, we *won't* lose heart.

REFLECTION QUESTIONS

- What enables you to be persistent in your church and community work? Where does that come from?

- How do you continue to pray and act without losing heart? Tell a story of one time when that happened.

REFLECTION FOUR

FROM "THE WORLD AS IT IS"
TO "THE WORLD AS IT SHOULD BE"

★ ★ ★ ★

ISAIAH 65:17-25

For I am about to create new heavens and a new earth; the former things shall not be remembered or come to mind. But be glad and rejoice forever in what I am creating; for I am about to create Jerusalem as a joy, and its people as a delight. I will rejoice in Jerusalem, and delight in my people; no more shall the sound of weeping be heard in it, or the cry of distress. No more shall there be in it an infant that lives but a few days, or an old person who does not live out a lifetime; for one who dies at a hundred years will be considered a youth, and one who falls short of a hundred will be considered accursed. They shall build houses and inhabit them; they shall plant vineyards and eat their fruit. They shall not build and another inhabit; they shall not plant and another eat; for like the days of a tree shall the days of my people be, and my chosen shall long enjoy the work of their hands. They shall not labor in vain, or bear children for calamity; for they shall be offspring blessed by the LORD—and their descendants as well. Before they call I will answer, while they are yet speaking I will hear. The wolf and the lamb shall feed together, the lion shall eat straw like the ox; but the serpent—its food shall be dust! They shall not hurt or destroy on all my holy mountain, says the LORD.

In community organizing we learn to act in the world as it is on behalf of the world as it should be. Engaging the world as it is, it's easy to get discouraged when faced with pervasive and growing problems in the world like poverty, homelessness, violence, war. Most of the time, it's hard to look at the world around us and feel like we are making any progress on any of these things. But when you break it down into a set of specific steps— five hundred units of housing here, seventy-five units of housing there—we begin to feel hopeful and encouraged. It's one of the things I like most about organizing.

Twenty members from our church once gathered with nearly five hundred members of the Washington Interfaith Network at First Rock Baptist Church in far Southeast DC. Together we celebrated progress we had made over the previous five years, especially the commitments the mayor had made to create and preserve affordable housing. The commitments were real and specific: five hundred new units of supportive housing for the homeless in downtown D.C.; seventy-five units of Nehemiah homes on Dix Street for new homeowners with incomes as low as $20,000 a year; immediate action to preserve affordable rental housing at 1483 Newton Street and 1020 Monroe in Columbia Heights; a pledge not to allow rent increases or condo conversions in buildings that have persistent code violations. It was not that all of our community's housing problems had gone away, but we had been given hope—indeed had given ourselves hope, as one of the speakers put it—to "keep on truckin'."

That was something of what the Prophet Isaiah was up to with the returning exiles in Jerusalem. The exiles had come home believing that immediately the Kingdom of David would be restored, the Temple rebuilt, and God's reign established once and for all on Mount Zion. Yet that's not how things worked out. Instead, they found a city in ruins and the rebuilding to be costly, painful, and dangerous. The task of the prophet was to keep Israel's hopes alive.

The task of the prophet was to keep Israel's hopes alive.

South African theologian John de Gruchy in his book *A New Heaven and a New Earth* suggests that there were three kinds of hope in the Old Testament following the exile. The first was Messianic, for the restoration of the Davidic monarchy. The King would be put back on the throne, and all would be right with the world. This hope, de Gruchy notes, was narrowly political: If we just get the right person in charge, elect the right leader, everything will work the way it's supposed to.

The second type of hope was apocalyptic. The world has gone so terribly wrong and is so utterly beyond redemption that only a wholesale destruction of the world as it is and a new world order established by God can provide any hope for the future. In our day, the "Left Behind" series embodies this sort of hope. A new day is coming, but only after everything we know has been destroyed. There's not much for us to do about it except wait for that great and terrible day to arrive...and hope we're among the few who are "raptured."

The third type of hope, de Gruchy suggests, is what we find in the Prophet Isaiah. It's not narrowly political nor is it pie-in-the-sky apocalypticism. It doesn't pin its hope on a single historic figure. Nor does it speak of catastrophic reordering of the world. Instead, it paints a vision of the world as it should be that is both concrete and specific, grounded in the real world as we know it. At the same time, the vision that Isaiah paints is beyond our capacity to create justice on our own. It is God who will bring this vision about, yet there is an invitation in Isaiah for us to be at work in the world, helping in whatever ways we can to create the new heaven and new earth that God will finally bring into being.

It is astonishing that Isaiah could pen these words twenty-five hundred years ago, and they still speak to our own immediate situation as well as they did to the exiles who first heard them in Jerusalem:

No more shall there be...
   an infant that lives but a few days,
   or an old person who does not
   live out a lifetime...
No more... shall they build houses
   and another inhabit them...
No more... shall they plant vineyards
   and another eat their fruit...
No more... shall they labor in vain,
   or bear children for calamity...

And then, the prophet declares...

The wolf and the lamb shall feed together,
   the lion shall eat straw like the ox...
They shall not hurt or destroy
   on all my holy mountain.

This is certainly not a description of the world as it is. We still live in a world where children die in infancy and the elderly languish in neglect, where the poor are exploited for their labor, and safe and decent housing for everyone is but a dream. In our work to create permanent supportive housing in our community, members of our congregation have worked with residents of the shelter where many of our city's homeless are warehoused in rooms where the bunks are so close together you can reach out from your bed to touch the bed across the aisle. And guess what? Most of the men who live at that shelter have jobs. The depressing state of housing in our nation's capital is that a person can work full-time on minimum wage and still not be able to afford a place to live. And here's the kicker: That particular shelter is just across K Street from some of the highest-priced lobbying firms in the nation.

If it's all up to God, there is not much for us humans to do except just sit on our hands and wait. If it's all up to us, on the other hand, we might as well give up hope right now. I am enough a product of the Reformed Tradition to know that even our best efforts are tainted with sin. Even community organizations, for all the good they do, sometimes sputter and die. The twentieth century was littered with the dashed hopes of one failed revolution after another, and the twenty-first hasn't started out all that well either.

When we imagine that justice is all up to us, we are especially prone to take violence into our hands to achieve our aims. The world at times makes progress in astonishing ways, but it is not inevitable, and history will record that Isaiah's hopes were never fully realized. Even in our best moments, human history takes at least a half-step back for every step forward. Yet Isaiah's vision of the world as it should be still beckons us forward. Now, just as much as then, we need to know that the future belongs to God.

De Gruchy writes further:

The future breaks into our present struggles, awakening hope and strengthening faith and love in the expectation that there is always more that God wants to give us. God is always ahead of us, always creating the new, always opening up new possibilities. So the true prophets are not awakening false expectations, but rather proclaiming that there is always more that God wants to give us, more that God wants to do. The prophets know that unless that hope of the more is kept alive, we will simply give up and begin to accept things as they are instead of reaching out to receive the more which God has in store for us.

Community organizing is born out of the conviction that God has yet more in store for us, and therefore we must refuse to accept things as they are. The reign of God will not come out of the work of our hands alone, but we are given glimpses of the Kingdom in the midst of our labors, and these glimpses are enough to sustain us and move us forward: residents from every sector of the city, working together across racial, religious, and economic divides in common cause to improve life in the city we call home.

Yes, the future belongs ultimately to God, but we are given a role to play and a foretaste of the future God has in store for us. This is holy work. It is God's work. Let us not be weary, therefore, in the task that is set before us.

REFLECTION QUESTIONS

- What, for you, symbolizes "the world gone wrong"? Make a list.

- What is your vision for "the world as it should be"? Make another list.

APPENDIX

GROUP STUDY GUIDE

★★★★

These four reflections can also be used for group Bible study as stand-alone sessions, as part of a weekend retreat, or over the course of several weeks. If participants have copies of the book, they can each read the reflections in advance. However, when the group gathers, begin with the Scriptures and not with this book. The purpose of these Bible studies is to engage the text directly and let the group draw its own conclusions.

Allow at least 45 minutes for each Bible study. Start them on time and end them at the time you promised.

The Bible study method is an adaptation of Walter Wink's *Transforming Bible Study*. There are three basic steps to this method. In the first step, participants try to get the story "into their gut" by acting it out, role-playing, or using some other method that helps bring the story alive. I find it particularly effective to tell the story "by heart" rather than read it aloud. Participants remember more of the details and enter the world of the story more quickly.

In the second step, the leader leads the group into the Biblical text by asking open-ended inductive questions. The questions do not seek right or wrong answers, but insight into the dynamic of the story.

The third step is to apply the passage to our own context by engaging in a creative "right brain" exercise.

In my experience, the setting of the room makes a great deal of difference. If possible, arrange the chairs in a circle. Light a candle in the center of the room as a symbol of the Holy Spirit's presence. I find it best to make a copy of the passage on a single sheet of paper, rather than passing out copies of the entire Bible. Begin with a time of singing, prayer, and a short silence.

During the silence, I often begin with a reflection question that begins to put the participants within the framework of the story. I usually begin by saying something like this:

> To help lead us into the text, I have prepared a series of questions. These are not "right or wrong" questions, but questions to help us wrestle with the dynamics of the story. Few of us feel like we are experts on the Bible, but all of us are experts on our own experience. My job is to keep us focused on the story; your job is to share what you see and experience. Think of the story as something that is at the center of the circle, bigger than all of us. It's not that we are all simply trying to give our own opinions, but that together we are trying to understand what the story has to teach. To do that, all of us need to wrestle with the story together. This story may be familiar to some of

you, but my invitation to you today is to try and listen to the story again as if for the first time.

★ ★ ★ ★

NOTES TO A LEADER

As a leader of this kind of discussion, it is important that you not simply follow the process woodenly, but work with the questions ahead of time to make them your own. Read the text through several times. See if you can learn it by heart and tell it from memory (you will be astonished when you do this how much of the text our mind tends to skip over when we read it). Look carefully at the questions and exercises I have provided, and then modify them so that you can ask them in your own voice and in a sequence that makes sense to you. Take your time with the process and don't rush. Resist the urge to answer your own questions. All of us begin with a sense of where the "payoff" of the story might be. However, if you trust the text, trust the questions, and trust the group, you will be surprised and rewarded with fresh insights that you had not anticipated.

The goal is not to impose an interpretation on the group, but, as Walter Wink puts it, to find "that subtle intersection between the text and our own life where the sparks fly, the insights are born, the corner is turned—where, in short, we find the living God addressing us at the point of our and the world's need."

MARK 6:30-44
From Crowd o Community

Focus Question During Silent Reflection: Remember a time in your life when you were tired, when things were so busy you barely had time to eat or sleep, when it felt as if everything depended on you.

Tell the story.

Pass out copies of the text.

Questions on the Text

1. This story immediately follows the story where Jesus sends the disciples out for the first time to teach and heal. They return, and Jesus invites them to go off to a deserted place by themselves. So, at the beginning, how do you imagine they are feeling about Jesus' invitation?

2. However, the crowd sees where they are going and gets there ahead of them. How do you imagine the disciples are feeling about Jesus' response to the crowd?

3. When it draws late, why do the disciples want to send the crowd away?

4. Why does Jesus respond, "You feed them"? What assumptions about the disciples' resources does Jesus hold that the disciples do not?

5. How do you think the disciples felt at Jesus' order? Why?

6. Why does Jesus ask the disciples to "go and see"? What assumptions about the crowd's resources does Jesus hold that the disciples do not?

7. Why do you think Jesus asks the disciples to have the crowd sit down in groups of 50?
   How does that change the dynamics? Is the size of the groups significant?

8. So what did the disciples learn? What did the crowd learn?

9. What does this story have to teach us about community organizing? About organizing inside our congregations?

10. In the story, the disciples are given the authority to organize the crowd in groups, to make them sit down. Who has that authority in our communities? What does it mean to have that authority?

11. Walter Brueggeman suggests that our culture lives by the myth of scarcity, while the gospel teaches us to live by the liturgy of abundance. Where do you see those tensions involved in the story? Where do you see that tension involved in your organizing work?

12. How would it change our internal and external organizing if we worked out of the liturgy of abundance, instead of the myth of scarcity?

Application Exercise

In a time of silence, give each participant a paper with a line vertical line drawn down the middle.

On the left side is written:

Fears of Scarcity

When I think about the work to which Jesus calls me, I worry that I do not have enough...

On the right side is written:

Gifts of Abundance

When I think about past situations to which I have been called to serve, I discovered to my surprise an abundance of...

Give participants ten minutes to complete the two lists with as many words as they can, and then five minutes to share their answers with a neighbor before reconvening the group. Ask each participant to say one thing that their "neighbor" said that really struck them.

End the session with, "This session made you realize... what?"

★★★★

EXODUS 3:1-9, 4:10-13
From Anger to Action

Focus Question During Silent Reflection: Remember a time in your life when you felt called to something, but you declined because you felt inadequate. Remember a time in your life when you felt called to something, felt inadequate, but did it anyway and discovered gifts you didn't know you had.

Tell the story.

Pass out copies of the text.

Questions on the Text

1. So, what's going on? What is the context? Why is Moses in the wilderness?

2. What does God say to Moses from the burning bush? Break it down. What does Moses learn about the God who speaks to him?

3. What, then, does God ask of Moses?

4. And Moses' response is what? To which God responds?

5. So why does Moses demure? Why does God push ahead?

6. What do we know about Moses before this story takes place?

7. Why might God have chosen Moses?

8. Organizers suggest that anger is an important quality of leadership. What do we know about Moses' anger? What does his anger tell us about Moses? Why might this matter to God in choosing Moses for this task?

9. Moses' plea to God, "O my Lord, please send someone else" is part of a pattern in the Old Testament of resistance to God's call, where those who are called cry "not up for the job." What do you make of this pattern?

Application Exercise

In a time of silence, hand each participant a paper with the following questions written on it and ask them to write their responses:

- What do you know of memory and grief in your own life over loss of what was taken away or the loss of potential for what might have been?

- How might God be speaking to you in that experience of anger?

- How in your life have you acted to change the situation that brought about the anger that you feel?

- How might God be calling you now through your anger to work for change?

Come back together after about ten minutes. Ask each participant to share one thing they wrote.

End the session with, "This session made you realize... what?"

★★★★

LUKE 18:1-8

From Pride to Perseverance

Focus Question During Silent Reflection: Remember a time in your life when you fought for something you believed in.

Tell the story.

Pass out copies of the text.

Questions on the Text

1. According to Luke, Jesus told this parable for what purpose?
2. So what do we know about the judge?
3. What do we know about the status of widows at the time Jesus is telling this parable?
4. What power does the judge have in this story? What power does the widow have?
5. What is the widow's demand?
6. How does the judge respond? What makes him relent?
7. According to Jesus, the lesson of the parable is what?
8. What does Jesus mean, "When the Son of Man comes, will he find such faith on earth?" What sort of faith is Jesus talking about?
9. If this were the only story we had to teach us about prayer, what sort of prayer does this story teach?

Application Exercise

Invite participants to practice a different posture for prayer. Instead of sitting, for example, stand. Instead of bowing your head, lift it up. Invite them to discover their "inner widow" and to silently lift up to God their most urgent prayer. Allow one or two minutes.

After the prayer, invite participants to share what it was like to pray in this way and what they prayed for. Ask the following question: How might your prayer affect the organizing work we do in the church and in the community?

End the session with, "This session made you realize... what?"

★ ★ ★ ★

ISAIAH 65:17-25
From "The World as It Is" to "The World As It Should Be"

Focus Question During Silent Reflection: In your church and community work, what for you symbolizes "the world gone wrong"? (For example, for me, it is the ten-foot hole in the track at Dunbar High School, ten blocks away from the Capitol.)

Tell the story.

Pass out copies of the text.

Questions on the Text

To set the context, it is helpful to also hand out a copy of Nehemiah 5:1-6. Explain that Nehemiah, along with Isaiah 65, is "post-exilic" literature, written after the Israelites have returned from the Babylonian exile. It was a difficult time with dashed expectations as the returned to Jerusalem to find the city in ruins. There were also inequalities between those who had stayed in Jerusalem (mostly the poor) and those returning (mostly the elite). There were accusations that the returnees—Jerusalem's new elite—were exploiting those who had stayed when the city was abandoned. Read Nehemiah 5:1-6 together.

1. What is Nehemiah describing? Does it have any relevance to what is going on today in our church and society?

2. In the Isaiah passage, who is the actor?

3. Why "new heavens and new earth"? Why "heavens" and not just "earth"?

4. Why forget the former things? What former things? Who is rejoicing? What does it mean for God to rejoice?

5. "No more" implies it is a present reality. Look at the "no mores."

6. What do "the sound of weeping and cries of distress" tell us?

7. What does it mean that infants live but a few days and the old do not live out their lifetimes?

8. Why mention infants and the elderly specifically?

9. Contrast "build and inhabit, plant and eat" with "build and another inhabit" and "plant and another eat." What's the difference? Who builds and plants for another? Who builds and plants for him or herself?

10. In contrast, what does it mean to enjoy the work of one's own hands?

11. What does it mean to labor in vain or to bear children in calamity?

12. The wolf and the lamb feed together, the lion eats straw like an ox; what is being pictured here? The only negative picture here is the serpent. Why a serpent?

13. South African theologian John de Gruchy suggests there are three types of post-exilic hope present in the Old Testament:

    a. The first is a "Messianic" hope for the restoration of the Davidic monarchy, a narrowly political hope;

b. The second is an "apocalyptic" hope that imagined the destruction of the old order, creation of a new order;

c. A third alternative is found in the text from Isaiah, a text which is neither narrowly Messianic nor full-blown apocalyptic.

14. Look at the first two alternatives:

a. Apocalyptic: This world is beyond redemption. What's the appeal? What's the problem with such hope?

b. Messianic: A new Martin Luther King. What's the problem with pinning our hopes on a singular figure? How is this text different? What is being pictured here?

15. De Gruchy suggests Isaiah's vision is not apocalyptic but rather is about this world. Yet the future is not all up to us. God is the principal actor. What happens to our hope when we imagine that it is entirely up to us?

16. De Gruchy suggests that the power of Isaiah's vision is that God is the actor, but the text leaves space for human participation. Where do you see it? What does this text require of us? What does it mean for us to live by such a vision?

17. As we organize in the "world as it is" on behalf of the "world as it should be," how does Isaiah's vision help us in our church and community work?

Application Exercise

In a time of silence, hand out a sheet of paper to each participant with the following written on it:

No more shall there be...

- For they shall...

- Invite each person to write his or her own ending to the two sentences. After five minutes, go around the table and invite each person to share his or her prophetic vision.

End the session with, "This session made you realize...what?"

★★★★

OTHER RESOURCES ON ORGANIZING

ACTION CREATES PUBLIC LIFE
by Edward T. Chambers

Ed Chambers, the successor to Saul Alinsky and an organizer for over 55 years, mulls about the need for human beings to develop their "Public life." He argues that it is by taking action that we define who we are as adults and help create the world-as-it-could-be. Written for those who want to participate in shaping society rather than sit around and complain about things.

35-page paperback, $5.95

THE POWER OF RELATIONAL ACTION
by Edward T. Chambers

Ed Chambers mulls about the building of relationships in public life that allow us to share our values, passions and interests with one another—what he calls "mixing human spirits." He describes the art of the relational meeting or "one-to-one," which he helped developed and which is now being used by clergy, leaders and organizers around the United States and in several other countries to build their congregations and community institutions and to take joint action for the common good.

33-page paperback, $5.95

THE BODY TRUMPS THE BRAIN
by Edward T. Chambers

The former executive director of the Industrial Areas Foundation (IAF) looks at how humans learn with all their senses—including instinct and intuition—and how our educations system tries to downplay what he calls "social knowledge" in favor of academic exercises.

48-page paperback, $5.95

OTHER RESOURCES ON ORGANIZING

REBUILDING OUR INSTITUTIONS
by Ernesto Cortes, Jr.
Ernie Cortes, the co-executive director of the Industrial Areas Foundation, argues that community organizing cultivates the practices needed for democracy to thrive, including one-on-one relational meetings, house meetings, and systematic reflection on them afterwards. This book contains several examples from organizations in California, Louisiana, and Texas that helped local congregations and other mediating institutions identify, confront, and change things that were destroying their families and communities.
30-page paperback, $5.95

EFFECTIVE ORGANIZING
FOR CONGREGATIONAL RENEWAL
by Michael Gecan
The author of *Going Public* and co-executive director of the Industrial Areas Foundation describes how the tools of organizing can and are transforming Protestant, Catholic, Jewish and Muslim congregations. Included are five case studies of congregations that have used this process to grow.
54-page paperback, $5.95

AFTER AMERICA'S MIDLIFE CRISIS
by Michael Gecan
Michael Gecan paints a vivid picture of civic, political, and religious institutions in decline, from suburban budget crises to failing public schools, what he describes as "a national midlife crisis." He shows how local organizational efforts can create vibrant institutions that truly serve their constituents and preserve and advance their communities.
128-page hardcover, $14.95